Simply Lamb

Quick & Easy Indian

Simply Lamb

Lustre Press
Roli Books

ISBN: 978-81-7436-800-3

For the recipes in this book we are grateful to Jeani Mohindra, Kalp Mithal, Purnima Kachru, Pushpesh Pant, Rita D'Souza, Sujit Bose, Vijaylakshmi Baig, and specially Rocky Mohan for recipies on pages 16, 48, 49, 52, 54, 78, 88 & 95.

Photographs: Deepak Budhraja, Dheeraj Paul, Sunny Singh

Published in India by Roli Books
in arrangement with Roli & Jansen BV
M 75 Greater Kailash II (Market),
New Delhi 110 048, India.
Phone: ++91-11-29212271, 40682000.
Fax: ++91-1129217185
Email: info@rolibooks.com
Website: www.rolibooks.com

Editor: Neeta Datta
Design: Supriya Saran
Pre press: Jyoti Dey

Printed and bound in China

Contents

Introduction

Meat plays an extremely important part in our diet. It supplies large quantities of high quality protein, iron, and several vitamins, especially those of the B group that are not easily available in other food. Apart from that, of course, most of us find a good appetizing meat dish one of the most satisfying meals.

TIPS ON BUYING MEAT

When choosing meat, it helps to bear in mind the cooking method that you intend using. If you are roasting or grilling meat, then a lean, tender cut is recommended. Slower cooking with added moisture such as *dum* is suitable for one of the tougher, probably fattier cuts. However, the nutritional quality of the latter is just as high as that of the dearer cuts and they will be just as tasty if cooked properly. Choose meat which has no undue amount of fat; what fat there is should be firm and free from dark marks or discolouration. Lean meat should be finely grained, firm and slightly elastic.

TIPS ON STORING MEAT

Put meat in the refrigerator as soon as possible after buying. Always store meat in the coldest part of the fridge. Remove any paper wrappings, rewrap the meat loosely in polythene or foil, leaving an end open for ventilation, and place the meat on a tray in case it drips. Most fresh meat can be stored in the refrigerator for up to 3-4 days. Minced and small cuts of meat are best eaten on the day you buy them or within one to two days. Joints and chops will keep for 2-3 days and large roasting joints for 5 days. Leaner cuts last longer than fatty cuts because fat gets rancid before meat. Never let the meat or its juices come into contact with other food in the fridge, particularly food that does not require any further cooking.

DIFFERENT CUTS OF LAMB

There are 5 major cuts of lamb: leg, loin, shoulder, rack and breast.

COOKING MEAT

There are two basic ways of cooking meat. The most tender cuts are best cooked quickly by dry heat such as roasting, grilling or sautéing which is using only a little moisture in the form of fat. Less tender cuts need added liquid and longer, slower cooking methods such as braising, pot roasting, stewing, and boiling.

Roasting: Meat is traditionally roasted in a hot oven – so that the joint is seared quickly. The flavour of the meat roasted by this process is excellent, but only the most tender cuts must be used. Roasting meat in foil or in a covered tin helps retain moisture, as well as keeps the oven clean, but the flavour and colour of the meat are not as good as it is if open roasted. Open the foil or remove the lid from the tin for the final 30 minutes of cooking to allow the outside of the meat to brown.

Grilling: This method is suitable only for the most tender cuts such as steaks or chops. Always grill under or over fierce heat, to sear the meat well on the outside first, then regulate the cooking by moving the grill rack further from the source of heat rather than by moderating the heat. Preheat a gas or electric grill for about 5 minutes before use. Or let the charcoal burn for 30 minutes if using the tandoor.

Sautéing: Many good quality cuts can be sautéed, if they are not too fatty. Use sufficient fat to cover the bottom of the pan. First brown the meat quickly on both sides on moderately high heat, then reduce heat and cook slowly till the meat is cooked through.

Braising: First the meat is browned quickly on all sides in a little fat in a frying pan. Then the liquid is added and the meat cooked, covered, slowly until tender. Flavouring vegetables are usually part of the dish and the cooking liquid is thickened to serve as a sauce.

Pot roasting: Similar to braising, this method is used for whole joints only. The meat is first browned and very little fat is added. The pan is then covered tightly and cooked till tender.

Boiling: Cover the tougher joints with cold water, bring to the boil and add flavouring ingredients. Cover the pan, reduce heat and simmer until tender.

Basic Preparations

BROWN ONION PASTE

Fry sliced onions on medium heat till brown. Drain the excess oil and allow to cool. Process until pulped (using very little water, if required). Refrigerate in an airtight container.

DHANSAK MASALA

Ingredient	Quantity
Coriander (*dhaniya*) seeds	1 kg / 2.2 lb
Cumin (*jeera*) seeds	250 gm / 9 oz
Turmeric (*haldi*)	1″ piece
Cinnamon (*dalchini*) sticks	50 gm / 1¾ oz
Cloves (*laung*)	50 gm / 1¾ oz
Black peppercorns (*sabut kali mirch*)	200 gm / 7 oz
White cardamom (*safed elaichi*)	50 gm / 1¾ oz
Mustard seeds (*rai*)	50 gm / 1¾ oz
Poppy seeds (*khus khus*)	50 gm / 1¾ oz
Curry leaves (*kadhi patta*)	50 gm / 1¾ oz
Black cumin (*shah jeera*) seeds	60 gm / 2 oz
Fenugreek seeds (*methi dana*)	50 gm / 1¾ oz
Bay leaves (*tej patta*)	50 gm / 1¾ oz
Dried orange peel (pith should be removed)	50 gm / 1¾ oz
Dried sweet lime peel (pith should be removed)	50 gm / 1¾ oz

Roast each ingredient individually with just 1-2 tsp oil on a griddle (*tawa*). Cool, grind and mix. Store in an airtight glass container. This can be kept for over a year.

GARLIC WATER

Mince 1½ tbsp garlic and mix with ¼ cup water. Let it stand for 5 minutes. Rub the mixture with your hands, through a fine muslin cloth, and collect the extract. Use as required.

COOKED YOGHURT

Whisk 2 cups / 500 gm / 1.1 lb yoghurt until very smooth. Add ½ cup water and whisk again to blend well. Pour this mixture into a round bottomed pan and cook on high heat. Stir constantly till the mixture comes to the boil. Then reduce heat to low, stirring occasionally, until the mixture is reduced to half its original quantity, and its colour has changed to off-white. Use as required in the recipe.

GHUSTABA

Take 500 gm / 1.1 lb fresh, boneless meat from the leg of lamb (with fat removed) and cut into 1" x 2" cubes. Mix 4 tbsp fat or unsalted butter, ¼ tsp green cardamom (*choti elaichi*) powder, and ¾ tbsp salt.

First pound the meat on a smooth stone with a wooden mallet. While pounding, remove any white tough fibre that may appear. Keep pounding until the meat changes colour.

Wet hands in chilled water, make balls with the meat paste, and keep aside for use for *ghushtaba*.

GARAM MASALA

Cumin (*jeera*) seeds	90 gm / 3 oz
Black peppercorns (*sabut kali mirch*)	70 gm / 2¼ oz
Black cardamom (*badi elaichi*) seeds	75 gm / 2½ oz
Fennel (*moti saunf*)	30 gm / 1 oz
Green cardamom (*choti elaichi*)	40 gm / 1¼ oz
Coriander (*dhaniya*) seeds	30 gm / 1 oz
Cloves (*laung*)	20 gm
Cinnamon (*dalchin*) sticks	20 x 205 cm
Mace (*javitri*) powder	20 gm
Black cumin (*shah jeera*) seeds	20 gm

Dry rose petals	15 gm
Bay leaves (*tej patta*)	15 gm
Ginger powder (*amchur*)	15 gm

Grind all the ingredients into a fine powder and store in an airtight container. Use as required.

GINGER / GARLIC PASTE

Soak 300 gm / 10 oz ginger / garlic cloves overnight to soften the skin. Peel and chop roughly. Process until pulped. The pulp can be stored in an airtight container and refrigerated for 4-6 weeks.

MINT CHUTNEY

Mint (*pudina*) leaves, chopped	60 gm / 2 oz
Green coriander (*hara dhaniya*), chopped	120 gm / 4 oz
Cumin (*jeera*) seeds	5 gm
Garlic (*lasan*) cloves	2
Green chilli, chopped	1
Raw mango, chopped	30 gm / 1 oz
Tomatoes, chopped	45 gm / 1½ oz
Salt to taste	

Blend all the ingredients until paste-like. Refrigerate in an airtight container. Use as required.

COCONUT MILK

Grate 1 coconut and press through a muslin cloth to obtain the first (thick) extract. Boil the grated coconut with equal quantity of water to obtain the second (thin) extract.

LAMB STOCK

Lamb	1 kg / 2.2 lb
Onions, medium-sized, chopped	2
Tomato, large, chopped	1
Water	4 cups / 1 lt / 32 fl oz
Salt	2 tsp / 6 gm
Turmeric (*haldi*) powder	a pinch
Ginger (*adrak*), chopped	1″ piece
Coriander (*dhaniya*) seeds	1 tbsp / 6 gm
Cinnamon (*dalchini*),	1″ stick 1
Cloves (*laung*)	4
Black peppercorns (*sabut kali mirch*)	10

Put the first 6 ingredients into a large pan. Tie the ginger and spices in a muslin cloth and add to the pan. Bring the mixture to the boil, lower heat and simmer for at least 1 hour. Skim off any scum. Squeeze the muslin bag to extract the flavours. Strain the stock. Remove the meat from the bones and keep aside. Refrigerate stock when cool and skim off any excess congealed fat, if desired.

Starters

Spicy and Aromatic Lamb Chunks

Shola Kebab

Serves: 4

INGREDIENTS

Lamb, cut into boneless pieces **900 gm / 2 lb**
Salt **3 tsp / 9 gm**
Red chilli powder **4 tsp / 12 gm**
White pepper (*safed mirch*) powder **a pinch**
Fenugreek (*methi*) powder **a pinch**
Green cardamom (*choti elaichi*) powder **a pinch**
Garam masala **2 tsp / 6 gm**
Onion (*kalonji*) seeds, crushed **2 tsp / 6 gm**
Fennel (*moti saunf*), crushed **a pinch**
Mustard seeds (*rai*), crushed **a pinch**
Cumin (*jeera*) seeds, crushed **a pinch**
Coriander (*dhaniya*) seeds, crushed **a pinch**
Ginger-garlic (*adrak-lasan*) paste **2 tbsp / 36 gm / 1¼ oz**
Raw papaya, grated **4 tbsp / 60 gm / 2 oz**
Mustard oil **½ cup / 100 ml / 3½ fl oz**
Vinegar (*sirka*) **4 tsp / 20 ml**
Yoghurt (*dahi*) **½ cup / 125 gm / 4 oz**
Butter for basting **4 tsp / 20 gm**

METHOD

Prepare the marinade by mixing all the ingredients (except butter) together.

Rub the mixture into the lamb pieces and keep aside for 1½ hours.

Skewer the lamb pieces and roast in a medium-hot tandoor for 10-12 minutes. Baste with butter and roast again for 5 minutes.

Remove from skewers and serve hot.

Cinnamon Flavoured Ribs

Ghar ke Chaamp

Serves: 6-8

INGREDIENTS

Lamb ribs, double **900 gm / 2 lb**
Ghee / Vegetable oil **½ cup / 100 gm / 3½ oz**
Onions, minced **3 cups**
Cinnamon (*dalchini*), 1" sticks **2**
Salt to taste
Sugar **2 tsp / 6 gm**
Red chilli power **1 tsp / 3 gm**
Malt vinegar (*sirka*) **½ cup / 125 ml / 4 fl oz**
Garam masala **1 tsp / 3 gm**

METHOD

Heat the ghee / oil in a deep-bottomed pan; add the onions and cinnamon sticks. Sauté until the onions become translucent. Add the ribs, stir and add 1 cup warm water, salt, sugar, red chilli powder, vinegar, and garam masala, and bring to the boil.

Reduce heat to low and cover the pan. Cook until the ribs are tender and very little gravy remains.

Lamb Steaks
Tandoori Masala Gosht

Serves: 4

INGREDIENTS

Lamb steaks (2x2) 8

For the marinade:

Onion, minced **1**

Garlic (*lasan*), crushed **1 tbsp / 18 gm**

Green chilli paste **1 tbsp / 15 gm**

Poppy seeds (*khus khus*), ground **1 tbsp / 15 gm**

Garam masala **1 tbsp / 7 gm**

Salt to taste

METHOD

For the marinade, mix onion, garlic, green chilli paste, poppy seed paste, garam masala, and salt together. Rub into the lamb steaks. Marinate for 2 hours.

Roast in a charcoal grill / tandoor till cooked as desired.

Serve hot, garnished with onion rings and accompanied by pickled green chillies.

Barbecued Lamb Liver and Kidney

Kallan Kebab

Serves: 4

INGREDIENTS

Lamb, minced **250 gm / 9 oz**
Lamb kidney, finely chopped **125 gm / 4 oz**
Lamb liver, finely chopped **125 gm / 4 oz**
Salt **½ tsp / 1½ gm**
Red chilli powder **2 tsp / 6 gm**
Garam masala **1 tsp / 3 gm**
Fenugreek (*methi*) powder a pinch
Ginger-garlic (*adrak-lasan*) paste **2 tsp / 12 gm**
Green coriander (*hara dhaniya*), chopped **1 tbsp / 4 gm**
Green chillies, chopped **1 tsp**
Chicken, minced **500 gm / 1.1 lb**
Salt **½ tsp / 1½ gm**
White pepper (*safed mirch*) powder **½ tsp / 1½ gm**
Garam masala **a pinch**
Fenugreek powder **a pinch**
Ginger-garlic paste **½ tsp / 3 gm**
Green coriander, chopped **1 tbsp / 4 gm**
Butter for basting **4 tsp / 20 gm**

METHOD

Mix the lamb mince, kidney, liver, salt, red chilli powder, garam masala, fenugreek powder, ginger-garlic paste, green coriander, and green chillies together. Keep aside.

Skewer the lamb mixture and roast in a charcoal grill for 8-10 minutes. Remove the skewer to allow excess moisture to drip off. Keep aside for 3-5 minutes.

Mix chicken with the remaining ingredients (except butter).

Apply a coat of the chicken mixture evenly over the lamb kebabs and roast for 5-6 minutes.

Baste with butter and remove the kebabs from skewers in 4 equal portions. Serve with green salad.

Minced Lamb Patties
Kheema na Pattice

Serves: 6-8

INGREDIENTS

Lamb, minced **750 gm / 26 oz**
For the filling:
Vegetable oil **2 tbsp / 30 ml / 1 fl oz**
Onions **2**
Ginger (*adrak*), 1" piece **1**
Garlic (*lasan*) cloves **6**
Green chillies, seeded **2**
Green coriander (*hara dhaniya*), chopped **½ cup / 12 gm**
Turmeric (*haldi*) powder **1 tsp / 3 gm**
Cumin (*jeera*) powder **2 tsp / 6 gm**
Salt to taste

Lemon (*nimbu*) juice **1 tbsp / 15 ml**
Potatoes, boiled, mashed **1½ kg / 3.3 lb**
Refined flour (*maida*) **5 tbsp / 50 gm / 1¾ oz**
Salt to taste
Vegetable oil **1 cup / 250 ml / 8 fl oz**
Eggs, beaten **4**
Breadcrumbs as required

METHOD

For the filling, heat the oil in a pan; sauté the onions till brown. Add the remaining ingredients and the lamb; sauté. Add a little water, if required, and cook till the lamb is brown and the mixture is completely dry.

Now, add the lemon juice. Mix well and keep aside to cool.

Mix the mashed potatoes with the refined flour and salt; knead well.

Take a spoonful of the potato mixture and flatten it with wet palms. Make a hollow in the centre and stuff 1½ tsp filling. Fold over the edges to seal the filling inside, and shape into a small round or oval cake. Repeat till all the cakes are done.

Heat the oil in a frying pan; dip each cake in the egg, coat with breadcrumbs and shallow-fry, turning over just once. Remove with a slotted spoon and drain the excess oil on absorbent paper towels. Repeat with the other cakes. Serve hot.

Succulent Lamb Chunks

Peshawari Kebab

Serves: 4

INGREDIENTS

Lamb, boneless, cut into
1" cubes **1 kg / 2.2 lb**

For the marinade:

Yoghurt (*dahi*) **½ cup / 120 gm / 4 oz**
Raw papaya paste **2 tsp / 10 gm**
Salt to taste
Red chilli powder **2 tsp / 6 gm**
Garam masala **1 tsp / 3 gm**
Black cumin (*shah jeera*) seeds
1 tsp / 2½ gm
Ginger (*adrak*) paste **1 tbsp / 18 gm**
Garlic (*lasan*) paste **1 tsp / 6 gm**

Ghee for basting
Chaat masala **1 tsp / 3 gm**
Juice of lemon (*nimbu*) **1**

METHOD

For the marinade, mix all the ingredients and rub well into the lamb. Leave aside for an hour.

Skewer the meat pieces and cook in a tandoor till half done.

Remove and leave to cool for 10 minutes.

Baste with ghee and cook for 8 more minutes.

Sprinkle with chaat masala and lemon juice. Serve hot with green salad.

Skewered Lamb Chops

Barah Kebab

Serves: 4

INGREDIENTS

Lamb, chops and leg pieces 900 gm / 2 lb

For the marinade:

Salt to taste

Red chilli powder 2 tsp / 6 gm

Garam masala 4 tsp / 12 gm

Malt vinegar (*sirka*) ¾ cup / 180 ml / 6 fl oz

Ginger (*adrak*) paste 3 tbsp / 54 gm / 1¾ oz

Garlic (*lasan*) paste 3 tbsp / 54 gm / 1¾ oz

Raw papaya paste 4 tsp / 20 gm or Kachri (*tenderizer*) 4 tsp / 20 gm

Black cumin (*shah jeera*) seeds 3 tbsp / 23 gm

Yoghurt (*dahi*) ¼ cup / 60 gm / 2 oz

Vegetable oil for basting

METHOD

For the marinade, mix all the ingredients together and rub into the lamb. Keep aside for 4 hours or overnight.

Skewer the pieces 1" apart and roast on slow fire in a tandoor or charcoal grill for 15 minutes or till half done.

Stand at room temperature for 20 minutes. Baste with oil.

Roast or grill on slow fire for another 20 minutes till velvety brown.

Serve with onion rings and lemon wedges.

Lamb Kebabs Stuffed with Cheese

Sakhat Kebab

Serves: 4

INGREDIENTS

Lamb, minced **900 gm / 2 lb**
Salt **1 tsp / 3 gm**
White pepper (*safed mirch*) powder **a pinch**
Red chilli powder **½ tsp / 1½ gm**
Fenugreek (*methi*) powder **a pinch**
Ginger-garlic (*adrak-lasan*) paste **2 tbsp / 36 gm / 1¼ oz**
Green chillies, chopped **1½ tsp**
Green coriander (*hara dhaniya*), chopped **1 tbsp / 4 gm**

For the filling:
Processed cheese, grated **120 gm / 4 oz**
Green chillies, chopped 4 tsp

For the batter:
Cornflour **7 tbsp / 70 gm / 2¼ oz**
Refined flour (*maida*) **7 tbsp / 70 gm / 2¼ oz**
Egg, whisked 1
Vinegar (*sirka*) **1 tsp / 5 ml**
Salt to taste
White pepper powder **a pinch**
Ginger-garlic paste **1½ tsp / 9 gm**
Water **1 cup / 250 ml / 8 fl oz**
Vegetable oil for frying

METHOD

Mix the lamb mince with the next 7 ingredients. Refrigerate for 15 minutes. Mix the filling ingredients together. Divide into 16 equal portions.

For the batter, mix all the ingredients (except oil).

Make 4″-long kebabs with the mince mixture and skewer in 4 equal parts. Roast for 5 minutes and remove. Allow to cool, remove from skewers in 4 pieces each.

Slit each kebab lengthwise and stuff the cheese mixture.

Dip the stuffed kebabs in the prepared batter and deep-fry in hot oil until crisp and golden brown.

Serve hot with mint chutney (see p. 11).

Bengali Style Lamb Cutlets

Mangsho Cutlet

Serves: 4

INGREDIENTS

Lamb, minced **500 gm / 1.1 lb**
Bread slices **2**
Garam masala **½ tsp / 1½ gm**
Onion, finely chopped **1**
Green chillies, finely chopped **4**
Mint (*pudina*) leaves **1 tsp**
Salt to taste
Eggs, whisked **8**
Breadcrumbs **½ cup / 60 gm / 2 oz**
Coriander (*dhaniya*) seeds **1 tsp / 2 gm**
Ghee **1¼ cups / 250 gm / 9 oz**

METHOD

Dip the bread slices in water, soaking them well. Remove and squeeze out all water.

Mix together the lamb mince, bread slices, garam masala, onion, green chillies, mint leaves, and salt. Keep aside for 1 hour.

Divide the mixture into 10 portions; shape into flat cutlets. Keep them aside on a tray.

Add salt to the eggs and stir.

Heat the ghee in a wok (*kadhai*); dip the cutlets in the egg mixture, then roll in the breadcrumbs and fry until golden brown. Drain the excess oil and serve.

Goan Crumb Fried Lamb Chops

Costeletas Empanados

Serves: 4

INGREDIENTS

Lamb chops **8 chops / 15 slices**

For the spice paste:

Green coriander (*hara dhaniya*) **1 cup / 25 gm**

Green chillies **2-3**

Garlic (*lasan*), minced **1 tsp / 6 cloves**

Ginger (*adrak*), minced **1 tsp / 1" piece**

Cumin (*jeera*) seeds **1 tsp / 2 gm**

Lemon (nimbu) juice **1½ tbsp / 22 ml**

Salt **1½ tsp / 4½ gm**

Black pepper (*kali mirch*) powder **¼ tsp**

Vegetable oil for shallow-frying

Refined flour (*maida*) **½ cup / 50 gm / 1¾ oz**

Eggs, beaten **2**

Breadcrumbs **1 cup / 120 gm / 4 oz**

METHOD

Beat the chops / slices with a rolling pin or meat mallet to tenderize.

For the spice paste, grind all the ingredients mentioned into a smooth paste. Apply the paste to the chops / slices and marinate for at least 2 hours.

Heat the oil in a frying pan. Roll the chops / slices in the flour, then dip in beaten eggs. Coat with breadcrumbs and fry for 5-7 minutes on each side till golden.

Serve hot, accompanied by a green salad or sautéed boiled potatoes.

Roasted Lamb Morsels

Boti Kebab

Serves: 4

INGREDIENTS

Lamb, cut into boneless pieces
1 kg / 2.2 lb
Ginger-garlic (*adrak-lasan*) paste ½ cup
Salt to taste
Lemon (*nimbu*) juice
5 tbsp / 75 ml / 2½ fl oz
Raw papaya paste 60 gm / 2 oz
Yoghurt (*dahi*), hung
¼ cup / 60 gm / 2 oz
White pepper (*safed mirch*) powder
1 tsp / 3 gm
Cumin (*jeera*) powder 1 tsp / 3 gm
Green cardamom (*choti elaichi*)
powder 1 tsp / 3 gm
Red chilli powder 2 tsp / 6 gm
Vegetable oil ½ cup / 125 ml / 4 fl oz
Butter for basting

METHOD

Marinate the lamb with ginger-garlic paste, salt, lemon juice, and raw papaya paste. Keep aside for 30 minutes.

Prepare a second marinade by mixing all the other ingredients except butter. Marinate the lamb cubes with this marinade and keep aside for 2 hours.

Skewer the lamb cubes and roast in a tandoor / oven / grill for 15-20 minutes. Remove, baste with butter and roast again for 3-5 minutes.

Remove from skewers and serve hot.

South Indian Style Lamb

Erachi Varatiyathu

Serves: 2-4

INGREDIENTS

Lamb, cut into cubes **250 gm / 9 oz**
Vegetable oil **2 tbsp / 30 ml / 1 fl oz**
Onions, big, sliced **3**
Red chilli powder **1 tsp / 3 gm**
Garam masala **1 tsp / 3 gm**
Turmeric (*haldi*) powder **¼ tsp**
Salt to taste
Tomatoes, chopped **2**
Sugar **1 tsp / 3 gm**
Juice of lemon (*nimbu*) **1**
Green coriander (*hara dhaniya*), chopped **2 tbsp / 8 gm**

Ground to a paste:

Green chillies **4**
Ginger (*adrak*) **1 tsp / 6 gm**
Garlic (*lasan*), pod **1**
Aniseed (*saunf*) **1 tsp / 2½ gm**
Coriander (*dhaniya*) powder **2 tsp / 6 gm**

METHOD

Heat the oil in a pan; add the onions, red chilli powder, garam masala, turmeric powder, and green chilli paste Sauté well.

Add the lamb and sauté till the oil separates. Add enough water to cook the lamb and still have a thick gravy.

When the lamb is almost done, add salt, tomatoes, sugar, and lemon juice. Cook till the lamb is tender. Serve hot, garnished with green coriander.

Skewered Lamb with Vegetables

Seekh Kebab Gilafi

Serves: 4

INGREDIENTS

Lamb, minced **1 kg / 2.2 lb**
Ginger (*adrak*) paste
3 tbsp / 54 gm / 1¾ oz
Brown onion paste (see p. 9)
1 cup / 300 gm / 11 oz
Green chillies, minced **6**
Garam masala **2 tsp / 6 gm**
Red chilli powder **2 tsp / 6 gm**
Salt **2 tsp / 6 gm**
Vegetable oil **3 tbsp / 45 ml / 1½ oz**
Processed cheese **¾ cup / 90 gm / 3 oz**
Onions, finely chopped
1 cup / 120 gm / 4 oz
Capsicum (*Shimla mirch*), finely chopped **100 gm / 3½ oz**
Tomatoes, deseeded, finely chopped
100 gm / 3½ oz
Butter for basting

METHOD

Mix the lamb mince with ginger paste, brown onion paste, green chillies, garam masala, red chilli powder, salt, oil, and processed cheese.

Mix together onions, capsicum, and tomatoes.

Squeeze out the excess water, if any, from the mince mixture and mix thoroughly. Keep aside for 2 hours.

Shape the mince mixture along the length of the skewers and coat with the vegetable mixture.

Roast in a tandoor / oven / grill for 10-15 minutes, basting with butter at regular intervals. Remove from skewers and serve hot.

INGREDIENTS

Lamb chops, cleaned, washed, pat dried **16**

For the first marinade: mix

Raw papaya paste for tenderizing **4″ x 4″**

Ginger-garlic (*adrak-lasan*) paste **1 tbsp / 18 gm**

Red chilli paste **1 tbsp / 15 gm**

Ginger juice **1½ tbsp / 25 ml**

Salt to taste

Vinegar (*sirka*) **2 tsp / 10 ml**

Vegetable oil **2 tsp / 10 ml**

For the second marinade:

Yoghurt (*dahi*), hung **1 cup / 250 gm / 9 oz**

Ginger-garlic paste **1 tbsp / 18 gm**

Ginger juice **4 tbsp / 60 ml / 2 fl oz**

Ginger, chopped **2½ tbsp / 15 gm**

Salt to taste

Garam masala **1 tbsp / 7 gm**

Yellow chilli powder **3 tsp / 9 gm**

Vegetable oil **5 tsp / 25 ml**

Melted butter for basting

Ginger Flavoured Lamb Chops

Adraki Champ

Serves: 4-6

METHOD

For the first marinade, mix all the ingredients together and apply over the lamb chops. Rub well and keep aside for 2-3 hours.

For the second marinade, whisk the hung yoghurt and add the remaining ingredients in the order listed. Mix well. Squeeze the extra moisture from the marinated chops and put them in this marinade. Keep aside for 3-4 hours.

Take a skewer and skew the marinated lamb chops, an inch apart, by piercing from the meat and along the bone so that it does not fall. Roast in a tandoor or over a charcoal grill at moderate temperature for 12-15 minutes. Hang the skewer to let the extra moisture drain off completely. Baste with melted butter and further roast for 4-6 minutes.

Serve hot with choice of salad and chutney.

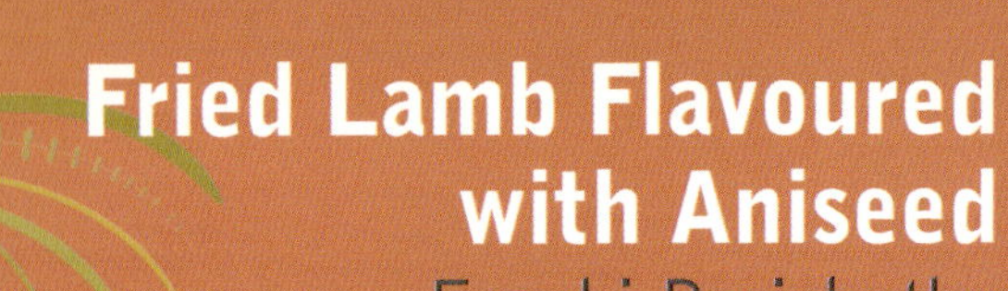

Fried Lamb Flavoured with Aniseed

Erachi Porichathu

Serves: 2-4

INGREDIENTS

Lamb, boneless **250 gm / 9 oz**
Aniseed (*saunf*) **2 tsp / 2½ gm**
Garlic (*lasan*), pod **1**
Salt to taste
Turmeric (*haldi*) powder **a pinch**
Red chilli powder **2 tsp / 6 gm**
Water **2 cups / 500 ml / 16 fl oz**
Vegetable oil for frying

METHOD

Grind the aniseed, garlic, and salt to a smooth paste. Marinate the lamb with the paste for half an hour. Keep aside.

In a non-stick pan, add the lamb, turmeric powder, and red chilli powder and cook over low heat for 45 minutes or till the water is completely absorbed and the lamb is tender. Keep aside.

Heat the oil in the wok (*kadhai*); deep-fry the lamb till golden brown.

Serve hot.

Satin Smooth Skewered Kebab

Kakori Kebab

Serves: 4-6

INGREDIENTS

Lamb, finely minced **750 gm / 26 oz**
Ginger-garlic (*adrak-lasan*) paste **1 tsp / 6 gm**
Cashew nut (*kaju*) paste **3 tbsp / 45 gm / 1½ oz**
Poppy seed (*khus khus*) paste **1 tbsp / 15 gm**
Salt to taste
Garam masala **1 tbsp / 7 gm**
Yellow chilli powder **1 tbsp / 7 gm**
Ghee **2 tbsp / 30 gm / 1 oz**
Melted butter for basting

METHOD

Mix the mince with all the ingredients mentioned (except butter). Divide the mixture into 16 equal portions and shape into balls.

Flatten each ball along the length of the skewer with moist hands.

Cook over charcoal grill at moderate temperature for about 5 minutes, rotating regularly to ensure even roasting.

Baste with melted butter and roast for another 1-2 minutes. Serve hot along with onion rings and chutney of your choice.

Classic Lamb Kebab

Shammi Kebab

Serves: 2-4

INGREDIENTS

Lamb mince 1 kg / 2.2 lb
Bengal gram (*chana dal*)
5 tbsp / 75 gm / 2½ oz
Red gram (*masoor dal*) 1½ tbsp / 25 gm
Black cardamom (*badi elaichi*) 3-4
Green cardamom (*choti elaichi*) 5-6
Dry red chillies (*sabut lal mirch*) 4-6
Cinnamon (*dalchini*), 1″ stick 1
Cloves (*laung*) 4-5
Black peppercorns (*sabut kali mirch*)
1½ -2 tsp / 6-8 gm
Ginger (*adrak*) 1″
Salt to taste
Green coriander (*hara dhaniya*),
chopped a large spring
Green chillies, chopped 2½ tbsp / 15 gm
Vegetable oil for shallow-frying

METHOD

Cook the mince with both the dals, whole spices, ginger, salt, and ½ cup water till the mixture becomes dry. Remove.

Discard the whole spices. Grind the mince to a fine paste. Add green coriander and green chillies. Mix well.

Divide the mixture into 20 equal portions and shape into flat patties with moist palms.

Shallow-fry the patties in oil till golden brown and crisp. Remove and serve hot.

Smoked Lamb Patties

Galauti Kebab

Serves: 4-6

INGREDIENTS

Lamb, minced thrice **750 gm / 26 oz**
Raw papaya paste
½ cup / 100 gm / 3½ oz
Roasted gram flour (*besan*)
4 tbsp / 40 gm / 1¼ oz
Salt to taste

Ghee for shallow-frying
For smoking:
Ghee **1 tbsp / 15 gm**
Green cardamom (*choti elaichi*), crushed 4

METHOD

Mix the mince and raw papaya paste together. Keep aside for 30 minutes. Add roasted gram flour and salt; mix.

For smoking, heat the ghee in a pan; add green cardamom and stir over low heat until red. Remove and when cool powder the seeds.

Put the mince in a large pan, make a hollow in the middle to place a metal bowl. Put a few pieces of live charcoal in this bowl. Sprinkle powdered seeds of green cardamom and 1 tbsp ghee on the charcoal, cover and smoke for 30 minutes. Uncover, remove the bowl.

Divide the mince into 12 equal balls and then flatten the ball between the palms into thick, round patties.

Shallow-fry the patties in ghee on a griddle (*tawa*) over low heat for 3-4 minutes, carefully turning once.

Goan Lamb Rissoles

Rissoís de Batata e Carne Picada

Serves: 6-8

INGREDIENTS

Lamb mince **500 gm / 1.1 lb**
Vegetable oil **4 tbsp / 60 ml / 2 fl oz**
Vegetable oil for frying
Onions, medium-sized, chopped **3**
Ginger (*adrak*), minced **3 tsp / 3″ piece**
Garlic (*lasan*), minced **2 tsp / 12 cloves**
Tomato, large, chopped **1**
Green chillies, minced **3**
Green coriander (*hara dhaniya*), chopped **3 tbsp / 12 gm**
Cumin (*jeera*) powder **1 tsp / 1½ gm**
Red chilli powder **1 tsp / 3 gm**
Black pepper (*kali mirch*) powder **½ tsp / 1½ gm**
Salt **1 tsp / 3 gm**
Vinegar (*sirka*) **2 tbsp / 30 ml / 1 fl oz**
Potatoes, medium-sized, boiled, mashed **6 / 750 gm / 26 oz**
Eggs, beaten **2**
Breadcrumbs **1 cup approx**

METHOD

Heat the oil in a pan; sauté the onions till golden. Add ginger and garlic; sauté for 1 minute.

Add the mince and fry on high heat for 5 minutes. Add the tomato, green chillies, green coriander, cumin powder, red chilli powder, black pepper powder, and salt; stir-fry. Add 1 cup hot water and bring to the boil, lower heat, and simmer covered for 10-15 minutes till done. Add vinegar and cook, uncovered, till dry.

Take 2" diameter balls of mashed potato seasoned with salt, hollow out and stuff with a little mince. Pinch together to seal. Pat into rounds, dip in egg, roll in breadcrumbs and shallow-fry till golden.

Main Course

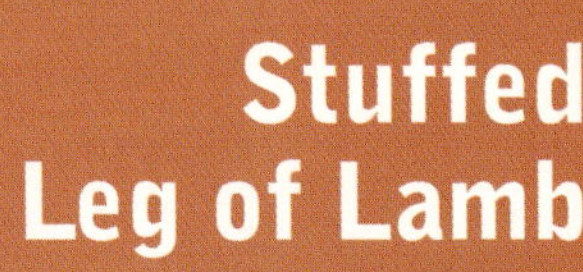

Stuffed Leg of Lamb

Raan-e-Dum

Serves: 4

INGREDIENTS

Leg of lamb **1 kg / 2.2 lb**
Red chilli powder **1 tsp / 3 gm**
Salt to taste
Ginger (*adrak*) paste **2 tsp / 12 gm**
Garlic (*lasan*) paste **2 tsp / 12 gm**
Malt vinegar (*sirka*) **5 tbsp / 75 ml / 2½ oz**
Spring onions, chopped **20 gm**
Ginger, chopped **150 gm / 5 oz**
Green chillies, chopped **10 gm**
Green coriander (*hara dhaniya*), chopped **2½ tbsp / 10 gm**
Mint (*pudina*), chopped **2 tsp**
Garlic, chopped **2½ tbsp / 30 gm / 1 oz**
Cheese, grated **60 gm / 2 oz**
Black cumin (*shah jeera*) seeds **1 tsp / 2½ gm**
Garam masala **½ tsp / 1½ gm**
White butter **5 tbsp / 100 gm / 3½ oz**
Onion rings **½ cup / 60 gm / 2 oz**
Pineapple, chopped **1 cup**
Chaat masala **1 tsp / 3 gm**
Lemon (*nimbu*) juice **1 tbsp / 15 ml**

METHOD

Remove the thigh bone from the lamb leg. Marinate the lamb in a mixture of red chilli powder, salt, ginger and garlic pastes, and half the malt vinegar. Keep aside for 4 hours.

Mix spring onions, ginger, green chillies, green coriander, mint, and garlic together. Add cheese and black cumin seeds. Stuff the leg of lamb with this mixture. Sew the open end of the leg with a needle and thread. Prick the leg with a fork.

Arrange the leg in a big baking tray. Pour over the remaining malt vinegar and sprinkle garam masala. Cover with aluminium foil. Roast in a preheated oven (180°C / 350°F) for 1½ hours.

Heat the butter in a pan; sauté the onion rings. Add pineapple and chaat masala. Mix well and remove from heat.

Slice the leg open and garnish with pineapple and onion mixture. Squeeze lemon juice on top and serve hot.

Tender Lamb in Thick Gravy

Kadhai Gosht

Serves: 2-4

INGREDIENTS

Lamb, cut into ½" cubes **500 gm / 1.1 lb**

For the marinade:

Red chilli powder **1 tsp / 3 gm**

Cumin (*jeera*) powder **1 tsp / 3 gm**

Coriander (*dhaniya*) powder **1 tsp / 3 gm**

Aniseed (*saunf*) powder **2 tsp / 6 gm**

Fenugreek (*methi*) leaves, fresh **2 tsp / 2 gm**

Yoghurt (*dahi*) **1 cup / 250 gm / 9 oz**

Vegetable oil **4 tbsp / 60 ml / 2 fl oz**

Onion, large, chopped **1**

Bay leaves (*tej patta*) **2**

Cinnamon (*dalchini*), 2" stick **1**

Cloves (*laung*) **6**

Green cardamom (*choti elaichi*) **6**

Ginger (*adrak*), finely chopped **1 tsp / 6 gm**

Garlic (*lasan*), finely chopped **1½ tsp / 6 gm**

Salt to taste

METHOD

In a big bowl, combine all the ingredients for the marinade (till yoghurt). Add the lamb, mix well and set aside to marinate for half an hour.

Heat the oil in a wok (*kadhai*); add the onion and sauté till translucent. Add bay leaves, cinnamon stick, cloves, green cardamom, ginger, and garlic. Stir thoroughly and fry for 2-3 minutes.

Add the marinated lamb and salt. Mix well. Pour 1 cup water and cook till the lamb is tender and the gravy is thick. Serve hot.

Tangy Lamb Cooked with Dried Plums

Alubukhara Korma

Serves: 4-6

INGREDIENTS

Hind leg of lamb, cut into pieces **1 kg / 2.2 lb**
Dried plums (*alubukhara*) **1 cup**
Water **12 cups / 3 lt / 96 fl oz**
Ghee **1 cup / 200 gm / 7 oz**
Green cardamom (*choti elaichi*) **8**
Cloves (*laung*) **4**
Salt to taste
Garlic water (see p. 9) **¼ cup / 60 ml / 2 fl oz**
Red chilli powder, dissolved in ½ cup water **2 tsp / 6 gm**
Cinnamon (*dalchini*), 2" sticks **4**
Tamarind (*imli*), boiled in 2 cups water for 10 minutes, strained **150 gm / 5 oz**
Turmeric (*haldi*) powder **2 tsp / 6 gm**

METHOD

Boil the water in a deep pan; add the meat and bring the water to the boil again. Boil for 2 minutes. Remove from heat and drain the water. Wash the meat in cold water and keep aside.

Put the meat in a pan and add ghee, green cardamom, cloves, salt, garlic water, red chilli water, and cinnamon sticks. Cook, stirring continuously, until the ghee separates from the masala.

Add just enough water so that when the meat is tender very little water remains. Cook covered till the meat is done. Add the tamarind extract, turmeric powder, and dried plums. Mix well, and simmer for 5-7 minutes, or till the plums are soft.

Lamb in Yoghurt Curry

Dhaniwal Korma

Serves: 4-6

INGREDIENTS

Leg of lamb, cut into pieces **1 kg / 2.2 lb**
Water **12 cups / 3 lt / 96 fl oz**
Ghee **1 cup / 200 gm / 7 oz**
Onion, puréed **¾ cup / 90 gm / 3 oz**
Garlic (*lasan*), ground **1 tsp / 6 gm**
Cloves (*laung*) **4**
Green cardamom (*choti elaichi*) **8**
Salt to taste
Saffron (*kesar*) **¼ tsp**
Cooked yoghurt (see p. 10) **1 cup / 250 ml / 8 fl oz**
Turmeric (*haldi*) powder **½ tsp / 1½ gm**
Coriander (*dhaniya*) powder **1½ tsp / 4½ gm**
Black pepper (*kali mirch*) powder **¼ tsp**
Green coriander (*hara dhaniya*), chopped **3 tbsp / 12 gm**

METHOD

Boil the water in a deep pan; add the meat and bring the water to the boil again. Blanch for 2-3 minutes and then drain the water. Cool the meat and wash under cold running water. Keep aside.

Put the blanched meat in a pan; add ghee, onion purée, garlic, cloves, green cardamom, salt, saffron, cooked yoghurt, turmeric and coriander powders. Mix well and cook until the ghee separates from the mixture.

Add just enough water so that when the meat is tender very little water remains. Sprinkle the black pepper powder and stir.

Serve hot, garnished with green coriander.

Shredded Lamb
Gosht ki Khurchan

Serves: 4

INGREDIENTS

Pasanda, boneless fillets from leg of lamb **500 gm / 1.1 lb**
Yoghurt (*dahi*), hung **2 tbsp / 30 gm / 1 oz**
Garlic-ginger (*lasan-adrak*) paste **1 tbsp / 18 gm**
Cumin (*jeera*) powder **1 tsp / 3 gm**
Red chilli powder **1 tsp / 3 gm**
Garam masala **1 tsp / 3 gm**
Vegetable oil **3 tbsp / 45 ml / 1½ fl oz**
Onion, medium-sized, finely sliced **1**
Green chillies, finely chopped **2**
Ginger, scraped, finely diced **1" piece**
Dry red chilli (*sookhi lal mirch*), shredded, optional **1**
Salt to taste

METHOD

Wash and pat dry the meat. Then with a sharp, heavy knife or small meat cleaver cut the *pasanda* into thin strips.

Blend the yoghurt and ginger-garlic paste with the powdered spices and marinate the *pasanda* strips in this mixture.

Heat the oil in a thick-bottomed frying pan and when it reaches smoking point lower heat and add the onion. When these begin to brown, add the meat with the marinade. Increase heat and stir-fry briskly for about 5 minutes. Use a large ladle to mash the meat at regular intervals as it cooks. Sprinkle green chillies and ginger along with the dry red chillies, if using. Lower heat and cook covered for another 5 minutes. Sprinkle a little water, if required. Remove when done to taste. Adjust the seasoning.

Serve accompanied with hot chapatti or *paratha* or on toast.

Pounded Lamb Balls in Yoghurt Gravy

Ghushtaba

Serves: 4

INGREDIENTS

Ghushtaba (see p. 10) **10**
Cooked yoghurt (see p. 10)
4 cups / 1 lt / 32 fl oz
Ghee **4 tbsp / 60 gm / 2 oz**
Stock, made with 4-5 bones boiled in 6 cups water, covered, for 45 minutes, strained **4 cups / 1 lt / 32 fl oz**
Green cardamom (*choti elaichi*) **8**
Black cardamom (*badi elaichi*) **6**
Cloves (*laung*) **6**
Fennel (*moti saunf*) powder **2 tsp / 6 gm**
Ginger powder (*sonth*) **2 tsp / 6 gm**
Garlic water (see p. 9)
¼ cup / 60 ml / 2 fl oz
Onion paste, fried **1 tbsp / 25 gm**
Salt to taste
Dry mint (*pudina*) leaves **¼ tsp**

METHOD

In a pan, add *ghushtaba*, cooked yoghurt, ghee, and stock; bring to a rapid boil. Add green and black cardamom, cloves, fennel powder, and ginger powder. Cover the pan and continue to boil for 10-12 minutes.

Add the garlic water and salt; boil for a further 10-12 minutes. Pour in more water, if required, to maintain a soup-like consistency. Add the onion paste and salt. Cook until the *ghushtaba* is tender to touch and the gravy has thickened.

Sprinkle the dry mint leaves and heat through.

Parsi Style Lamb in Tomato Gravy

Rus Chawal

Serves: 4

INGREDIENTS

Lamb, cut into pieces 750 gm / 26 oz
Vegetable oil ½ cup / 125 ml / 4 fl oz
Onions, large, finely sliced lengthwise 3
Ginger-garlic (*adrak-lasan*) paste 2 tsp / 12 gm
Red chilli powder 1 tsp / 3 gm
Turmeric (*haldi*) powder ¼ tsp
Salt to taste
Tomatoes, large, finely sliced 4
Potatoes, peeled, cut lengthwise 250 gm / 9 oz
Green coriander (*hara dhaniya*), finely chopped 1 tbsp / 4 gm

METHOD

Heat the oil in a large pan; add the onions and sauté till brown. Add the ginger-garlic paste, red chilli powder, turmeric powder, and salt; sauté for about 1 minute.

Add the tomatoes and let the mixture simmer till it is absolutely dry.

Add the lamb and sauté for some time. Gradually, add about 3 cups water and cook till the lamb is almost done. Add the potatoes and cook till tender.

Garnish with green coriander and serve hot with steamed rice.

Lamb in Rich Spicy Gravy

Roganjosh

Serves: 4

INGREDIENTS

Lamb, washed well **1 kg / 2.2 lb**
Yoghurt (*dahi*), whisked
1 cup / 250 gm / 9 oz
Cloves (*laung*) **4**
Cinnamon (*dalchini*), 2" stick **1**
Black cardamom (*badi elaichi*) **3**
Bay leaves (*tej patta*) **2**
Ghee **¾ cup / 150 gm / 5 oz**
Salt to taste
Asafoetida (*hing*) **a pinch**
Red chilli powder **2 tsp / 6 gm**
Water **2 cups / 500 ml / 16 fl oz**
Ginger powder (*sonth*) **2 tsp / 6 gm**
Aniseed (*saunf*) powder **4 tsp / 12 gm**
Saffron (*kesar*), optional **½ tsp**
Garam masala **1 tsp / 3 gm**

METHOD

Marinate the lamb in yoghurt, cloves, cinnamon stick, black cardamom, and bay leaves mixture for 10 minutes.

Heat the ghee in a deep pan; add the lamb and cover till it stops spattering. Add salt and asafoetida; stir.

Cook on high heat till the yoghurt dries. Lower heat and stir briskly to prevent from sticking.

Sprinkle a little water and stir till the meat browns. Repeat this twice, cooking till the oil separates.

Add the red chilli powder mixed with a little water. Cook on high heat, stirring briskly. Add water, ginger powder, and aniseed powder; cook for 15 minutes.

Soak the saffron in 4 tsp of hot water; grind and add to the lamb. Cook until the lamb is tender and the oil separates. Sprinkle garam masala and serve hot.

Lamb Morsels Cooked with Tomatoes

Kadhai Maas

Serves: 4-6

INGREDIENTS

Lamb, boneless pieces **1 kg / 2.2 lb**
Vegetable oil **1 cup / 250 ml / 8 fl oz**
Tomatoes, red, pulpy, blended **1 kg / 2.2 lb**
Water **2-3 tbsp / 30-45 ml / 1-1½ fl oz**
Salt to taste
Green chillies, large, cut into ¾" pieces **250 gm / 9 oz**

METHOD

Heat the oil in a wok (*kadhai*); add the tomatoes and cook till the oil separates, stirring continuously.

Add the lamb and cook till it is almost tender, stirring and adding little water occasionally to prevent it from sticking to the bottom.

When the lamb is almost tender, add the salt and green chillies.

Cook till the green chillies are soft and the lamb is dry.

Serve hot.

Lamb with Chickpeas – Bengali Style

Mangsho Ghugni

Serves: 2-4

INGREDIENTS

Lamb, boneless pieces 200 gm / 7 oz
Chickpeas (*kabuli chana*) 100 gm / 3½ oz
Vegetable oil 5½ tbsp / 80 ml / 2¾ fl oz
Onions, chopped ¼ cup / 30 gm / 1 oz
Ginger (*adrak*) paste 1 tsp / 6 gm
Garlic (*lasan*) paste 1 tsp / 6 gm
Tomatoes, chopped 50 gm / 1¾ oz
Red chilli powder ½ tsp / 1½ gm
Coriander (*dhaniya*) powder ½ tsp / 1½ gm
Cumin (*jeera*) powder ½ tsp / 1½ gm
Water 1 cup / 250 ml / 8 fl oz
Green coriander (*hara dhaniya*), chopped 1 tbsp / 4 gm

METHOD

Soak the chickpeas in water overnight; next morning boil till soft.

Heat the oil in a pan; add the onions, ginger and garlic pastes, tomatoes, and lamb. Mix well.

Add all the spice powders and water; cook till the lamb is done.

Add the chickpeas along with the water in which they were boiled. Bring the mixture to the boil. Remove from heat and serve hot, garnished with green coriander.

Lamb Cooked with Lentils and Vegetables

Dhansak

Serves: 6-8

INGREDIENTS

Lamb, cut into small pieces **1 kg / 2.2 lb**
Vegetable oil **3 tbsp / 45 ml / 1½ fl oz**
Onions, finely chopped **3**
Ginger-garlic (*adrak-lasan*) paste
2 tbsp / 36 gm / 1¼ oz
Dhansak masala (see p. 9)
2 tbsp / 20 gm
Lentil (*masoor dal*), washed
¼ cup / 50 gm / 1¾ oz
Split red gram (*arhar dal*)
1 cup / 200 gm / 7 oz
Green gram (*sabut moong dal*)
¼ cup / 50 gm / 1¾ oz
Bengal gram (*chana dal*)
¼ cup / 50 gm / 1¾ oz
Red pumpkin (*lal kaddu*), chopped
50 gm / 1¾ oz
Aubergine (*baingan*), small, chopped **1**
Tomatoes, small, chopped **2**
Onion, big, chopped **1**
Potato, chopped **1**
Fenugreek (*methi*) leaves,
fresh **2 tbsp / 10 gm**
or Dry fenugreek leaves (*kasoori methi*)
1 tsp / ½ gm

METHOD

Wash and soak the lentil and red and green grams separately for 1 hour. Drain and keep aside.

Heat the oil in a pan; sauté the onions, ginger-garlic paste, and *dhansak masala* till brown.

Pressure cook the lamb, lentil, grams, vegetables, and onion mixture with adequate water till the meat is done. Keep aside to cool.

Remove the meat pieces; mash and strain the remaining mixture. Then cook for 5-7 minutes. Now add the meat and cook till the mixture becomes thick.

Serve hot.

Bengali Lamb Curry
Kosha Mangsho

Serves: 2-4

INGREDIENTS

Lamb leg, cut into pieces
500 gm / 1.1 lb
Yoghurt (*dahi*) ¾ cup / 180 gm / 6 oz
Salt 3 tsp / 9 gm
Turmeric (*haldi*) powder 1 tsp / 3 gm
Ghee ¾ cup / 150 gm / 5 oz
Onions, chopped ½ cup / 60 gm / 2 oz
Garam masala 2 tsp / 6 gm
Ginger (*adrak*) paste 4 tsp / 24 gm
Garlic (*lasan*) paste 4 tsp / 24 gm
Coriander (*dhaniya*) powder
4 tsp / 12 gm
Cumin (*jeera*) powder 3 tsp / 9 gm
Red chilli powder 2 tsp / 6 gm
Tomatoes, chopped 60 gm / 2 oz

METHOD

Marinate the lamb with yoghurt, salt, and ½ tsp turmeric powder for 30 minutes.

Heat the ghee in a wok (*kadhai*); add the onions and garam masala (keep ½ tsp aside for garnishing). Cook for 10 minutes.

Add the marinated lamb. Cook for 10-12 minutes.

Add ginger and garlic pastes, coriander powder, cumin powder, red chilli powder, the remaining turmeric powder, and tomatoes. Cover and simmer till the lamb is tender.

Serve hot, with ½ tsp garam masala powder sprinkled on top.

Fried Ribs Garnished with Silver Leaves

Kabargah

Serves: 4

INGREDIENTS

Lamb ribs, 3" x 5" pieces **1 kg / 2.2 lb**
Milk **2 cups / 500 ml / 16 fl oz**
Black cardamom (*badi elaichi*), crushed **3**
Cinnamon (*dalchini*), 1" sticks **2**
Cloves (*laung*) **4**
Bay leaves (*tej patta*) **2**
Garam masala **1 tsp / 3 gm**
Asafoetida (*hing*) **a pinch**
Salt **2 tsp / 6 gm**
Ghee **1½ cups / 300 gm / 11 oz**
Yoghurt (*dahi*) **½ cup / 125 gm / 4 oz**
Red chilli powder **½ tsp / 1½ gm**
Silver leaves (*varq*) **5-6**

METHOD

Put the ribs in a pot; add milk, black cardamom, cinnamon sticks, cloves, bay leaves, garam masala, asafoetida, and salt. Cook till the milk gets absorbed.

Remove from heat, and transfer the ribs to a large plate. Keep aside.

Heat the ghee. Meanwhile, whisk together the yoghurt, red chilli powder, and a little salt until smooth in consistency.

Dip each rib into the yoghurt and fry to a rich brown colour. Drain excess oil and transfer to a serving dish.

Garnish with silver leaves and serve hot, as a snack or as part of the main course.

Spicy Lamb in Thick Gravy

Rara Meat

Serves: 4

INGREDIENTS

Lamb, pieces **1 kg / 2.2 lb**
Ghee **1 cup / 200 gm / 7 oz**
Onion paste **1½ cups / 450 gm / 1 lb**
Ginger (*adrak*) paste **4 tsp / 24 gm**
Garlic (*lasan*) paste **4 tsp / 24 gm**
Cinnamon (*dalchini*), 1" stick **1**
Cloves (*laung*) **3**
Tomato purée **1 cup / 250 ml / 8 fl oz**
Red chilli powder **4 tsp / 12 gm**
Turmeric (*haldi*) powder **1 tsp / 3 gm**
Coriander (*dhaniya*) powder **3 tsp / 9 gm**
Nutmeg (*jaiphal*), ground **½**
Mace (*javitri*), ground **1 tsp / 3 gm**
Yoghurt (*dahi*) **1 cup / 250 gm / 9 oz**
Salt to taste
Garam masala **2 tsp / 6 gm**
Green coriander (*hara dhaniya*), finely chopped **½ cup / 30 gm / 1 oz**

METHOD

Heat the ghee in a wok (*kadhai*) on medium-high heat. When hot, add the onion paste and fry till it turns light brown in colour.

Add ginger-garlic pastes and sauté for a few seconds.

Add cinnamon stick, cloves, and lamb. Cook till the lamb is slightly tender and brown. Add tomato purée, red chilli powder, turmeric powder, coriander powder, nutmeg, mace, yoghurt, and salt. Cook for 10 minutes more on medium heat.

Add garam masala and 3 cups water. Cook covered on low heat until the oil separates from the spices and comes to the surface.

The lamb should be quite tender by now. Remove the cover and let it simmer for 5-6 minutes, until enough of the liquid has evaporated, leaving a thick gravy.

Serve hot, garnished with green coriander.

Dry and Pungent Lamb

Chokhta

Serves: 6-8

INGREDIENTS

Lamb, cleaned and cut 1 kg / 2.2 lb
Water 1 cup / 250 ml / 8 fl oz
Vegetable oil ½ cup / 125 ml / 4 fl oz
Salt to taste
Asafoetida (*hing*) 2 pinches
Red chilli powder 2 tsp / 6 gm
Ginger powder (*sonth*) 1½ tsp / 4½ gm

METHOD

Cook the lamb in a heavy-bottomed pot with the water, oil, salt, and asafoetida. Cook covered, on high heat, for 20 minutes. Stir occasionally to ensure that it gets evenly done.

When the liquid dries and the oil surfaces, lower the flame and cook till it is deep brown in colour and a little crisp to touch, stirring continuously.

Add red chilli powder mixed in a few spoons of water and stir briskly on high heat till it becomes a rich red colour.

Add a few spoons of water and the ginger powder. Stir briskly, on high heat, till the oil surfaces. Remove and serve accompanied with plain rice.

Note: *This is a spicy and pungent dish. Vary the quantity of red chilli powder and ginger powder to suit your taste.*

Pickled Lamb Chops

Gosht Achaari Chaamp

Serves: 6-8

INGREDIENTS

Lamb chops, on 2 bones **8 pieces**
Raw papaya **a small piece**
Ginger (*adrak*) paste **2 tsp / 12 gm**
Garlic (*lasan*) paste **2 tsp / 12 gm**
Salt to taste
Gram flour (*besan*) **2 tsp / 10 gm**
Aniseed (*saunf*) **1 tsp / 3 gm**
Black cardamom (*badi elaichi*) **1 tsp / 3 gm**
Black pepper (*kali mirch*) powder **1 tsp / 3 gm**
Cloves (*laung*) **1 tsp / 3 gm**
Mustard oil **¼ cup / 60 ml / 2 fl oz**
Mustard seeds (*rai*) **1 tsp / 3 gm**
Onion seeds (*kalonji*) **1 tsp / 1½ gm**
Red chilli powder **2 tsp / 6 gm**
Yoghurt (*dahi*), whisked **¼ cup / 60 gm / 2 oz**
Chaat masala **1 tsp / 3 gm**
Lemon (*nimbu*) juice **1 tbsp / 15 ml**

METHOD

Flatten the chops with a steak hammer. Rub the chops with the papaya, ginger-garlic paste, and salt; keep aside.

Roast the gram flour in a pan till light brown and sprinkle over the lamb chops.

Mix the remaining ingredients with the yoghurt to a fine batter. (Do not add chaat masala or lemon juice.)

Marinate the chops in this marinade for 2 hours.

Preheat the oven to 180°C / 350°F.

Skewer the chops and roast in a hot tandoor or oven until cooked.

Remove the chops from the skewers. Sprinkle with chaat masala and lemon juice and serve.

Tangy Liver
Kaleji Masala

Serves: 4

INGREDIENTS

Liver, sliced 500 gm / 1.1 lb
Garlic (*lasan*) paste 2 tsp / 12 gm
Ginger (*adrak*) paste 2 tsp / 12 gm
Cinnamon (*dalchini*), 2" stick 1
Green chillies 4-5
Black peppercorns (*sabut kali mirch*) 8-10
Cumin (*jeera*) seeds 1 tsp / 2 gm
Malt vinegar (*sirka*) ½ cup / 125 ml / 4 fl oz
Sugar ½ tsp / 1½ gm
Salt to taste
Ghee ½ cup / 100 gm / 3½ oz
Onions, finely sliced 1¾ cups / 175 gm / 5¾ oz
Tomatoes, large, finely chopped 2

METHOD

Put the liver in some water, add garlic paste, ginger paste, and cinnamon stick. Boil for about 10 minutes. Remove the pieces from the stock, wash and keep aside. Collect the residual stock for later use.

Prepare the marinade by mixing all the remaining ingredients except the last three. Apply this mixture on the liver pieces and keep aside for about 10 minutes.

Heat the ghee in a pan; add the onions, and sauté until golden brown. Add salt, liver with the marinade, and the stock. Bring to the boil. Add the tomatoes and cook till the water dries up.

Shallow Fried Liver Cubes

Talli Kaleji

Serves: 6-8

INGREDIENTS

Liver (*kaleji*), cleaned (membranes removed), cut into 1" pieces 1 kg / 2.2 lb
Salt to taste
Grind to a paste:
Ginger (*adrak*), 2" piece 1
Garlic (*lasan*) cloves 8
Dry red chillies (*sookhi lal mirch*) 6
Turmeric (*haldi*) powder 1 tsp / 3 gm
Cumin (*jeera*) seeds 1 tsp / 2 gm
Vegetable oil 3 tbsp / 45 ml / 1½ fl oz

METHOD

Marinate the liver with the ground paste and salt.

Heat the oil in a pan; shallow-fry the liver for 2-3 minutes. Do not over fry as the liver will get tough.

Serve hot.

Lamb Cooked with Whole Spices

Khada Masala Gosht

Serves: 6

INGREDIENTS

Lamb, cut into pieces **1 kg / 2.2 lb**
Vegetable oil **½ cup / 125 ml / 4 fl oz**
Onions, finely chopped **2**
Fennel (*moti saunf*) seeds **1 tsp / 2½ gm**
Coriander (*dhaniya*) powder **1 tsp / 3 gm**
Cumin (*jeera*) powder **1 tsp / 3 gm**
Cloves (*laung*) **8**
Cinnamon (*dalchini*), 2″ stick **1**
Green cardamom (*choti elaichi*) **5**
Ginger (*adrak*) paste **1 tbsp / 18 gm**
Garlic (*lasan*) paste **1 tbsp / 18 gm**
Salt to taste
Yoghurt (*dahi*) **1 cup / 250 gm / 9 oz**
Garam masala **½ tsp / 1½ gm**

METHOD

Heat the oil in a pan; add the onions, sauté till light brown. Add the whole and powdered spices, lamb, ginger paste, garlic paste, salt, and yoghurt; mix well.

Cover with a thick lid that can hold about 1 cm of water on it, and cook over low heat for 2 hours.

Remove the lid and continue to cook if you want the preparation to be dry.

Add garam masala, mix well and serve hot.

Note: *This is dum pukht style of cooking. The lamb cooks in its own juices and as long as there is water on the lid, the ingredients inside the pan will never burn.*

INGREDIENTS

Lamb with bones, cut into small pieces
1 kg / 2.2 lb
Ghee 2 tbsp / 30 gm / 1 oz
Onion, sliced 1
Cinnamon (*dalchini*), 1″ sticks 2
Bay leaves (*tej patta*) 2
Onion, chopped 1
Black cardamom (*badi elaichi*) 3
Cloves (*laung*) 5
Coriander (*dhaniya*) powder 2 tsp / 6 gm
Red chilli powder 1 tsp / 3 gm
Turmeric (*haldi*) powder ½ tsp / 1½ gm
Garlic (*lasan*) paste 2½ tsp / 15 gm
Ginger (*adrak*) paste 2″ piece
Salt to taste
Yoghurt (*dahi*), beaten
1 cup / 250 gm / 9 oz
Refined flour (*maida*) 1 tsp / 3 gm
Gram flour (*besan*) 2 tsp / 6 gm
Garam masala 1 tsp / 3 gm
Mace (*javitri*), powdered ½ tsp / 1½ gm
Aniseed (*saunf*), powdered
1 tsp / 2½ gm
Green cardamom (*choti elaichi*),
powdered 5
Saffron (*kesar*) a few strands
Lemon (*nimbu*) juice 1 tbsp / 15 ml
Green coriander (*hara dhaniya*)
4 tbsp / 32 gm / 1 oz
Vetivier (*kewda*) essence (optional)
2 tsp / 10 ml

Lamb in Smooth Flavourful Gravy

Nihari Gosht

Serves: 6

METHOD

Heat the ghee in a pan; add the sliced onion, cinnamon sticks, and bay leaves; sauté on medium heat until golden brown. Add the lamb, chopped onion, black cardamom, and cloves; cook till the liquid has evaporated.

Add the coriander powder, red chilli powder, turmeric powder, garlic paste, ginger paste, and salt; sauté until the oil separates.

Add the yoghurt and bring the mixture to the boil. Reduce heat to medium and cook for about 15 minutes.

Add 2 cups water and bring to the boil again, cover and simmer, stirring occasionally, until the lamb is tender. Remove the lamb from the gravy and keep aside.

Heat 1 tbsp ghee in a pan; add the refined flour and gram flour; sauté over low heat, stirring constantly until light brown. Stir in the gravy. Strain the thick gravy through a soup strainer, reheat the gravy and bring to the boil.

Add the lamb, garam masala, mace powder, aniseed powder, green cardamom powder, saffron, and lemon juice; mix well and cook over low heat for 30 minutes.

Vetivier essence is added just before serving, but it is optional.

Garnish with green coriander and serve with tandoori roti or *naan*.

Lamb in Thick Lentil Gravy

Kala Masoor Dal Ma Gosht

Serves: 6-8

INGREDIENTS

Lentil (*masoor dal*), washed, soaked for 1 hour **250 gm / 9 oz**
Lamb, cut into pieces **750 gm / 26 oz**
Vegetable oil **2 tbsp / 30 ml / 1 fl oz**
Onions, large, chopped lengthwise **3-4**
Ginger-garlic (*adrak-lasan*) paste **2 tbsp / 36 gm / 1¼ oz**
Garam masala **1 tsp / 3 gm**
Parsi sambhar masala **1 tsp / 3 gm**
Green chillies, whole **4**
Turmeric (*haldi*) powder **½ tsp / 1½ gm**
Salt to taste
Tomatoes, finely chopped **3-4**

METHOD

Heat the oil in a large pan; sauté the onions till golden brown. Add the ginger-garlic paste, garam masala, Parsi *sambhar* masala, green chillies, turmeric powder, and salt. Sauté for 5-10 minutes.

Add the tomatoes and cook over low heat till the water is completely absorbed.

Add the lamb and the drained lentil; pressure cook till 3 whistles or till done.

Take out a bowlful of lentil from the cooker, mash well and put it back in the cooker. (This is done for a smooth gravy.)

Serve hot.

Variation: *This dish can also be made without lamb.*

Parsi Lamb with Dried Apricots

Jardaloo Ma Gosht

Serves: 4-6

INGREDIENTS

Lamb, cut into pieces **500 gm / 1.1 lb**
Dried apricots (*khubani*), deseeded, soaked for **4 hours 250 gm / 9 oz**
Vegetable oil **2 tbsp / 30 ml / 1 fl oz**
Onions, chopped **2-3**
Garlic (*lasan*) cloves, ground to paste **6-8**
Ginger (*adrak*), 2″ piece, ground to paste **1**
Salt to taste
Cinnamon (*dalchini*), 2″ stick **1**
Sugar to taste

METHOD

Heat the oil in a wok (*kadhai*); sauté the onions till golden brown. Add the ginger-garlic paste and sauté for 5-8 minutes.

Add the lamb, salt, and cinnamon stick. Sauté for a few minutes. Add enough water to cook the lamb till tender.

In another pan, brown the sugar. Add the apricots with the soaked water. Bring the mixture to the boil. Lower heat and cook till the apricots turn soft.

Mix the apricot mixture with the cooked lamb. Heat again and serve hot.

Lamb with Vegetables in Coconut Milk

Lamb Stew

Serves: 6

INGREDIENTS

Lamb / Chicken, tender **1 kg / 2.2 lb**
Vegetable oil **¼ cup / 60 ml / 2 fl oz**
Cinnamon (*dalchini*), 1″ sticks **3**
Cloves (*laung*) **12**
Green cardamom (*choti elaichi*) **4**
Black peppercorns (*sabut kali mirch*), crushed **1½ tbsp**
Onions, sliced long **½ cup / 60 gm / 2 oz**
Green chillies, slit half **6**
Ginger (*adrak*), sliced long **1½ tbsp / 36 gm / 1¼ oz**
Garlic (*lasan*) cloves **15**
Curry leaves (*kadhi patta*) **a few**
Refined flour (*maida*) **1 tbsp / 10 gm**
Vinegar (*sirka*) **2¼ tbsp / 33 ml / 1 fl oz**
Coconut milk, thick, extracted from 2 cups of grated coconut **½ cup / 100 ml / 3½ fl oz**
Coconut milk, thin **3 cups / 600 ml / 16½ fl oz**
Potatoes, carrots, beans, and peas **1 cup**
Black peppercorns **12**

METHOD

Sauté the whole spices in oil. Add the next 5 ingredients. Sauté for a while; remove and keep aside. In the same oil, sauté the flour. Add the meat and fry slightly. Add 1½ tbsp vinegar, salt, and thin coconut milk.

When the meat is half cooked, add the vegetables and onion mixture. Cook covered till the gravy is reduced. Add the remaining vinegar and the thick coconut milk. Bring to the boil and remove from heat. Add the black peppercorns and serve hot.

Red Hot Lamb Curry

Lal Maas

Serves: 4-6

INGREDIENTS

Lamb, cut into pieces 1 kg / 2.2 lb
Vegetable oil 1½ cups / 375 ml / 13 fl oz
Red chilli powder 6 tsp / 18 gm
Coriander (*dhaniya*) powder ¼ cup
Onions, sliced 3
Yoghurt (*dahi*) 1 cup / 250 gm / 9 oz
Salt to taste
Turmeric (*haldi*) powder 1 tsp / 3 gm
Garlic (*lasan*) paste
2 tbsp / 36 gm / 1¼ oz
Water, lukewarm
2 cups / 500 ml / 16 fl oz
Green coriander (*hara dhaniya*), chopped 1 tbsp / 4 gm

METHOD

Mix together all the ingredients from red chilli powder to turmeric powder (except garlic paste) and marinate the lamb pieces for one hour.

Heat the oil in a heavy-bottomed pan; add the lamb pieces and cook for 45 minutes over low heat till the pieces become tender.

Add the garlic paste and cook till the oil separates.

Add the water and bring to the boil. Garnish with green coriander and serve with hot *bajra roti*

No-Fuss Rajasthani Lamb

Junglee Maas

Serves: 4-6

INGREDIENTS

Lamb, cut into pieces **1 kg / 2.2 lb**
Vegetable oil **1½ cups / 375 ml / 13 fl oz**
Salt to taste
Water ½ **cup / 125 ml / 4 fl oz**
Red chilli powder **4-5 tbsp**

METHOD

Heat the oil in a heavy-bottomed deep pot. Add the lamb, salt, and water.

Cook covered on high heat, till it is heated through.

Lower heat and cook for 30 minutes; ensuring that the lamb does not stick to the bottom of the pot. Add the red chilli powder and cook till the lamb is tender.

Serve hot.

Lamb Curry Cooked in Milk

Aab Gosht

Serves: 6-8

INGREDIENTS

Lamb, cut into pieces **1 kg / 2.2 lb**
Water **4 cups / 1 lt / 32 fl oz**
Aniseed (*saunf*) powder **5 tsp / 15 gm**
Garlic (*lasan*) cloves, crushed **5**
Ginger powder (*sonth*) **1 tsp / 3 gm**
Salt to taste
Milk **4 cups / 1 lt / 32 fl oz**
Green cardamom (*choti elaichi*), split open **6**
Brown Onion paste (see p. 9) **1 tbsp / 25 gm**
Black pepper (*kali mirch*) powder **1 tbsp / 6 gm**
Ghee **½ cup / 100 gm / 3½ oz**

METHOD

Boil the lamb in water with the aniseed powder, garlic, ginger powder, and salt till it is tender. Remove the lamb and keep aside. Strain the stock in another pan and keep aside.

In a separate pan, boil the milk with green cardamom. Simmer till the milk is reduced to half. Add fried onion paste, black pepper powder, and ghee. Mix well.

Add the lamb and the stock. Stir well and bring the mixture to the boil. Continue to boil for 5-7 minutes and then reduce the heat to low and simmer for another 10 minutes.

Serve hot.

Lamb in Spinach Sauce

Saag Meat

Serves: 2-4

INGREDIENTS

Lamb, cut into pieces 500 gm / 1.1 lb
Spinach (*palak*), chopped 300 gm / 11 oz
Ghee ½ cup / 100 gm / 3½ oz
Onions, chopped 1 cup / 120 gm / 4 oz
Ginger (*adrak*) paste 2 tsp / 12 gm
Garlic (*lasan*) paste 2 tsp / 12 gm
Coriander (*dhaniya*) powder 2 tsp / 6 gm
Red chilli powder 2 tsp / 6 gm
Turmeric (*haldi*) powder 1 tsp / 3 gm
Cumin (*jeera*) seeds 1 tsp / 3 gm
Garam masala 1 tsp / 2 gm
Yoghurt (*dahi*) ½ cup / 125 gm / 4 oz
Salt 2 tsp / 6 gm

METHOD

Heat the ghee in a wok (*kadhai*); add the onions and sauté till light brown.

Add ginger-garlic pastes and sauté for a while. Now, add the lamb and cook for 10 minutes.

Add coriander powder, red chilli powder, turmeric powder, cumin seeds, garam masala, yoghurt, and salt. Cook for 15 minutes.

Finally, add the spinach and cook over low heat till the spinach has wilted, the lamb is tender and there is hardly any liquid left.

Serve hot with a dash of ghee.

Tangy Lamb Mince

Achras

Serves: 4

INGREDIENTS

Lamb, coarsely minced **750 gm / 26 oz**
Ghee ½ **cup / 100 gm / 3½ oz**
Onions, chopped **2 cups / 240 gm / 9 oz**
Garlic (*lasan*) paste **1 tsp / 6 gm**
Ginger (*adrak*) paste **2 tsp / 12 gm**
Coriander (*dhaniya*) powder **1 tbsp / 7 gm**
Red chilli powder **1½ tsp / 4½ gm**
Turmeric (*haldi*) powder **½ tsp / 1½ gm**
Salt to taste
Raw mangoes (*kairi*), medium-sized, diced **2**
Ginger, 1½" chopped, 1½" cut into juliennes **3"**
Green chillies, deseeded, chopped **6**
Mint (*pudina*), chopped **1½ tsp**
Black peppercorns (*sabut kali mirch*), freshly roasted, coarsely ground **½ tsp / 2 gm**
Clove (*laung*) powder **a small pinch**
Black cardamom (*badi elaichi*) powder **a small pinch**

METHOD

Melt the ghee in a pan; add onions and stir-fry until translucent.

Add the garlic and ginger pastes and stir-fry until onions are golden.

Put in coriander, red chilli and turmeric powders (dissolved in ¼ cup water) and continue to stir-fry until fat the leaves the sides.

Now add the mince, stir-fry until light brown. Add salt and water (approx. 1½ cups) and stir-fry until fat leaves the sides.

Add raw mangoes, chopped ginger, green chillies, and mint; mix well, cover with a lid and keep aside (the heat of the cooked mince will soften the raw mangoes) for 10 minutes.

Uncover and adjust the seasoning. Sprinkle black pepper, clove and black cardamom powders, cover with a lid again until ready to serve. Garnish with ginger juliennes.

INGREDIENTS

Lamb, boneless, cut into cubes
900 gm / 2 lb
Vegetable oil **150 ml / 5 fl oz**
Cinnamon (*dalchini*), 1″ sticks **2**
Cloves-Green cardamom
(*laung-choti elaichi*) **5**
Nutmeg (*jaiphal*), powdered **1**
Ginger-garlic (*adrak-lasan*) paste
2 tbsp / 36 gm / 1¼ oz
Onions, chopped **1 cup / 120 gm / 4 oz**
Salt **1½ tsp / 4½ gm**
Red chilli powder **1 tsp / 3 gm**
Coriander (*dhaniya*) powder **1 tsp / 3 gm**
Turmeric (*haldi*) powder **1 tsp / 3 gm**
Carrots (*gajar*), cut into rounds
200 gm / 7 oz
Tomato purée, fresh
1 cup / 200 gm / 7 oz
Wholemilk fudge (*khoya*) **30 gm / 1 oz**
Brown onion paste (see p. 9)
3 tbsp / 45 gm / 1½ oz
Green peas (*hara matar*), shelled
100 gm / 3½ oz
Mushrooms (*guchhi*), stems removed
80 gm / 2¾ oz
Cashew nuts (*kaju*), whole
½ cup / 60 gm / 2 oz
Yoghurt (*dahi*) **2½ tbsp / 50 gm / 1¾ oz**
Garam masala **2 tsp / 6 gm**
Water **4 cups / 1 lt / 32 fl oz**

Boneless Lamb Cooked in a Pot

Baoli Handi

Serves: 4

METHOD

Heat the oil in a pot; add cinnamon sticks, cloves, green cardamom, and nutmeg; sauté till they crackle. Add ginger-garlic paste and sauté again for a few more minutes.

Add lamb and onions. Cook over medium heat till the liquid dries. Add salt, red chilli powder, coriander powder, turmeric powder, and carrots.

Stir in tomato purée and cook till the oil separates.

Mix in wholemilk fudge, brown onion paste, green peas, mushrooms, cashew nuts, yoghurt, and garam masala. Add water and cover the dish with a layer of dough. Reduce heat and cook till the meat is tender and the gravy has thickened.

Serve hot accompanied with steamed rice.

Braised Lamb in Aromatic Gravy

Qorma Shahi

Serves: 4-6

INGREDIENTS

Lamb, shanks, chops **1 kg / 2.2 lb**
Vegetable oil **1 cup / 250 ml / 8 fl oz**
Onions, finely sliced **500 gm / 1.1 lb**
Almonds (*badam*) **50 gm / 1¾ oz**
Green chillies, chopped **4**
Bay leaves (*tej patta*) **2**
Ginger (*adrak*), chopped **1 tbsp / 7½ gm**
Garlic (*lasan*), chopped **1 tbsp / 6 gm**
Coriander (*dhaniya*) powder **2 tsp / 6 gm**
Garam masala **1 tsp / 3 gm**
Salt to taste
Red chilli powder **2 tsp / 6 gm**
Yoghurt (*dahi*), made from full-cream milk **3 tbsp / 45 gm / 1½ oz**
Mace (*javitri*) powder **¼ tsp**
Green cardamom (*choti elaichi*) **powder ¼ tsp**
Saffron (*kesar*) **a few strands**
Vetiver (*kewda*) essence Or Rose water (*gulab jal*) **1 tsp / 5 ml**

METHOD

Heat half the oil in a pan; fry the onions until light brown. Add the almonds and continue to fry until the onions are deep brown. Remove, cool and grind to a fine paste.

In the same pan, heat the remaining oil and lightly stir-fry the green chillies, bay leaves, ginger, garlic, coriander powder, and ½ tsp garam masala along with the lamb and salt for 10 minutes stirring continuously.

Reduce heat, add red chilli powder and yoghurt; mix well and continue to cook for 3-4 minutes. Simmer until there is hardly any moisture left.

Add the fried onion-almond paste and mix well. Sprinkle the remaining garam masala, mace and green cardamom powders and fry for a couple of minutes more. Add about 4 cups water and cook until the lamb is tender. Sprinkle saffron soaked in vetiver essence or rose water just before serving.

INGREDIENTS

Lamb, cut into pieces **1 kg / 2.2 lb**
Salt to taste
Yoghurt (*dahi*) **1 cup / 250 gm / 9 oz**
Ghee **1 cup / 200 gm / 7 oz**
Green cardamom (*choti elaichi*) **6-8**
Cloves (*laung*) **5-6**
Cinnamon (*dalchini*), 1″ sticks **3-4**
Onions, big, sliced **3**
Ginger (*adrak*), 3″ pieces, shredded **2**
White peppercorns (*sabut safed mirch*), powdered **15-20**
Red chilli seeds, powdered **2 tbsp / 30 gm / 1 oz**
Poppy seeds (*khus khus*), ground **2 tbsp / 40 gm / 1¼ oz**
Coconut (*nariyal*), powdered **2 tbsp / 30 gm / 1 oz**
Wholemilk fudge (*khoya*), grated **½ cup / 100 gm / 3½ oz**
Almonds (*badam*), blanched, chopped **15**
Cashew nuts (*kaju*) **10**
Garlic (*lasan*), ground to paste **3 pods**
Saffron (*kesar*) **a pinch**
Milk **1 tbsp / 15 ml**
Dry red chillies (*sookhi lal mirch*), deseeded **6-8**

Exotic Rajasthani Lamb Curry

Safed Maas

Serves: 4-6

METHOD

Boil the lamb in water with 2 tbsp salt for 10 minutes.

Discard the water and transfer the lamb pieces onto a flat dish. Smear the pieces with yoghurt.

Heat the ghee; add green cardamom, cloves, cinnamon, and onions. Fry till the onions turn translucent. Add ginger and fry for 1-2 minutes.

Add the lamb pieces, white peppercorns, and red chilli seeds. Cook for 45 minutes, over low heat.

Add the poppy seeds and coconut powder; simmer for 15-20 minutes. Add the wholemilk fudge and stir the lamb.

Add almonds and cashew nuts and then cook until the lamb is almost done.

Add garlic paste. Cook over low heat till done.

Add saffron soaked in 1 tbsp milk; mix well. Garnish with deseeded skins of red chillies and serve.

Masala Lamb in Yoghurt Sauce

Gosht Falaknuma

Serves: 4

INGREDIENTS

Lamb, cubed, boneless **500 gm / 1.1 lb**
Ghee / Vegetable oil **½ cup / 100 gm / 3½ oz**
Ginger (*adrak*) paste **2 tsp / 12 gm**
Garlic (*lasan*) paste **2 tsp / 12 gm**
Salt to taste

For the masala:
Onions, sliced **¾ cup / 90 gm / 3 oz**
Red chilli powder **1 tsp / 3 gm**
Garam masala **2 tsp / 6 gm**
Treacle or brown sugar, dissolved in 2 tbsp water **1 tbsp / 15 gm**
Green chillies, thinly sliced **5 / 15 gm**
Almonds (*badam*), blanched, peeled and ground to a paste **25 / 20 gm**
Yoghurt (*dahi*), hung in a muslin cloth for at least 2 hours and then whisked **3 cups / 750 gm / 26 oz**
Green coriander (*hara dhaniya*), fresh, chopped **1 tbsp / 4 gm**
Saffron (*kesar*), dissolved in 4 tbsp of hot water **½ tsp / ½ gm**

METHOD

Heat half the ghee / oil in a pan; add ginger and garlic pastes and cook until golden in colour. Add the lamb and salt. Stir and add just enough water which will dry when the lamb becomes tender.

For the masala, heat the remaining ghee / oil in a frying pan; add the onions and sauté until golden in colour. Add red chilli powder, garam masala, treacle water, green chillies, and almond paste. Add ½ cup water and cook until the water dries up completely.

Reheat the cooked lamb and add the masala to it. Stir, add yoghurt and green coriander. Mix well, add the saffron and simmer until the oil comes to the surface.

Leg of Lamb in Creamy White Sauce

Chandi Kaliya

Serves: 4

INGREDIENTS

Leg of spring lamb **1 kg / 2.2 lb**
White butter **150 gm / 5 oz**
Green cardamom (*choti elaichi*) **10**
Yoghurt (*dahi*), whisked
1 cup / 250 gm / 9 oz
Salt to taste
Cream **½ cup / 120 ml / 4 fl oz**
Black pepper (*kali mirch*) to taste
Green cardamom powder **1 tsp / 3 gm**
Silver leaves (*varq*) for decoration

For the chandi paste: Blend with 3 tbsp water to a smooth paste

Garlic (*lasan*), peeled **30 gm / 1 oz**
Onions, chopped **100 gm / 3½ oz**
Green chillies, slit, deseeded **8-10**
Almonds (*badam*), blanched, peeled **20**

METHOD

Melt the butter in a pot (*handi*); add green cardamom and stir over low heat for 30 seconds. Add the *chandi* paste and stir for about 5 minutes.

Add lamb, yoghurt, salt, and 3 cups water; cover and simmer, stirring occasionally, until tender. Increase heat to medium, add cream and bring to the boil. Sprinkle black pepper and green cardamom powder; stir.

Serve hot decorated with silver leaves.

Lamb in Yoghurt Coriander Sauce

Salan Dahiwala

Serves: 4-6

INGREDIENTS

Lamb (*raan or hind leg*) **1 kg / 2.2 lb**
Ghee **1½ cups / 300 gm / 3½ oz**
Cloves (*laung*) **4**
Ginger powder (*sonth*) **1 tsp / 3 gm**
Asafoetida (*hing*) **a pinch**
Ginger (*adrak*), chopped **2″**
Yoghurt (*dahi*) **1 cup / 250 gm / 9 oz**
Red chilli powder **1 tsp / 3 gm**
Turmeric (*haldi*) powder **1 tsp / 3 gm**
Mango powder (*amchur*) **4 tsp / 12 gm**
Coriander (*dhaniya*) powder **1 tsp / 3 gm**
Garam masala **2 tsp / 6 gm**
Green coriander (*hara dhaniya*), chopped **500 gm / 1.1 lb**
Salt to taste

METHOD

Heat the ghee in a tinned pot (*degchi*); add the cloves, ginger powder, asafoetida, ginger, lamb, yoghurt, red chilli and turmeric powders, and water. Cook for 30 minutes, constantly adding 1-2 tbsp water to prevent burning.

When the lamb is tender and a little gravy remains, add mango, coriander and garam masala powders, green coriander, and salt. Cook for 10 minutes more over low heat. Remove and serve.

Lamb Cooked with Bengal gram

Dal Gosht

Serves: 6-8

INGREDIENTS

Lamb, cut into ½" cubes **1 kg / 2.2 lb**
Bengal gram (*chana dal*), soaked for 2 hours **1 cup / 200 gm / 7 oz**
Vegetable oil **4 tbsp / 60 ml / 2 fl oz**
Ginger-garlic (*adrak-lasan*) paste **4 tsp / 24 gm**
Turmeric (*haldi*) powder **1 tsp / 3 gm**
Red chilli powder **2 tsp / 6 gm**
Garam masala **2 tsp / 6 gm**
Onions, chopped, paste **3**
Tomatoes, chopped, paste **4**
Salt to taste
Sugar **1 tsp / 3 gm**
Yoghurt (*dahi*) **1 cup / 250 gm / 9 oz**
Green coriander (*hara dhaniya*), finely chopped **1 tbsp / 4 gm**

METHOD

Drain and cook the Bengal gram in 1 cup water till tender, but not over cooked. Drain and keep aside.

Heat the oil in a wok (*kadhai*); add the lamb and fry till well browned. Add the ginger-garlic paste, turmeric powder, red chilli powder, garam masala, and onion-tomato pastes. Reduce heat and cook till the oil separates from the mixture.

Add the salt, sugar, yoghurt, and 2½ cups water. Cook over low heat till the lamb is tender. Add the Bengal gram and bring the mixture to the boil. Lower heat and simmer until well blended.

Serve hot, garnished with green coriander.

Lamb with Black Pepper and Coconut Milk

Gosht Lazeez

Serves: 6-8

INGREDIENTS

Lamb, cut into pieces **1 kg / 2.2 lb**
Ghee / Vegetable oil
¾ cup / 150 gm / 5 oz
Dry red chillies (*sookhi lal mirch*) **4**
Onions, chopped
1½ cups / 180 gm / 6 oz
Ginger (*adrak*) paste **2 tsp / 12 gm**
Red chilli powder **1 tsp / 3 gm**
Turmeric (*haldi*) powder **½ tsp / 1½ gm**
Coriander (*dhaniya*) powder **2 tsp / 6 gm**
Salt to taste
Garlic (*lasan*) paste, added to **¾ cup** warm water **2 tsp / 12 gm**
Coconut (*nariyal*) milk, thick
2 cups / 400 ml / 14 fl oz
Black peppercorns (*kali mirch*), coarsely ground to a powder **1 tsp / 3 gm**
Lemon (*nimbu*) juice **1 tbsp / 15 ml**

METHOD

Heat the ghee / oil in a heavy-bottomed vessel; add dry red chillies. Fry until they are almost black in colour, then add onions. Sauté until translucent. Add the ginger paste and stir-fry for a minute. Add the red chilli powder, turmeric powder, coriander powder, and salt.

Add the lamb and stir and roast with the garlic water until the water is absorbed. The lamb should be brown in colour.

Add the coconut milk to ½ cup warm water and cook over low heat until the lamb becomes tender and the gravy thickens.

Add the black pepper powder and lemon juice. Stir and heat thoroughly.

Index

STARTERS

MAIN COURSE